Carving Egg People

Mary Finn

Text written with and photography by Donna S. Baker

4880 Lower Valley Road, Atglen, PA 19310 USA

Ten Basic Steps

Below are ten basic steps for making an "egg person." They are guidelines, an outline to help you. The steps suggest a progression or an order toward completion to help with your carving. Use the ten basic steps to aid you in making your own "egg people" once you have tried some of the samples in the book. Have fun and good luck!

1) ESTABLISH THE HEAD

2) SHAPE THE FACE

3) HAIR

4) DRAW THE BODY

5) MAKE THE BACK OF THE ARMS

6) MAKE THE FRONT OF THE ARMS

7) LEGS (if you want them)

8) CLOTHING/COSTUME

9) DETAILS

10) PAINT OR STAIN, THEN APPLY A FINISH

Designed by John P. Cheek
Type set in ZapfHumanist Dm BT

ISBN: 0-7643-1313-4
Printed in China

Dedication

To my family for their unending love and support today and always. Thank you! Also to three great individuals who helped my husband Stan and I in a time of great need. Brad Windorl and Mike helped us when our trailer was sideswiped and "totaled" by a truck. They called for help and kept our dogs in their car with the air conditioning running while we sorted things out with the emergency crew. Related to the same incident, A. Charles (Chuck) Artinian helped us by first allowing Stan, me, and the three dogs to stay in his ARA Motel, although dogs are normally not allowed. Later that day, he lifted our spirits (which were very down) at his fantastic restaurant, The Corn Crib, located in Gap, Pennsylvania. Thank you for what you did for us in our time of great need.

Published by Schiffer Publishing Ltd.
4880 Lower Valley Road
Atglen, PA 19310
Phone: (610) 593-1777; Fax: (610) 593-2002
E-mail: Schifferbk@aol.com
Please visit our web site catalog at
www.schifferbooks.com
We are always looking for people to write books on new and related subjects. If you have an idea for a book, please contact us at the above address.

This book may be purchased from the publisher.
Include $3.95 for shipping.
Please try your bookstore first.
You may write for a free catalog.

In Europe, Schiffer books are distributed by
Bushwood Books
6 Marksbury Avenue
Kew Gardens
Surrey TW9 4JF England
Phone: 44 (0) 20 8392 8585
Fax: 44 (0) 20 8392 9876
E-mail: Bushwd@aol.com
Free postage in the UK. Europe: air mail at cost.

Contents

Introduction

Our family loves to camp and we spend much of the spring, summer, and fall enjoying this passion. Since space is limited and you can't take a band saw with you to cut out blanks, I had to come up with a fun and easy way to have lots of projects available. Many of my students had the same problem for one reason or another, such as living in an apartment, not having access to saws and other large equipment, and so forth. Thus I came up with the idea of carving wooden eggs. They worked very well for teaching students to carve faces (see my first book, *Carving Egg Heads*), so the jump to other projects was an easy reach.

Each egg has the potential to become a friend or relative while creating lots of fun and enjoyment for the carver. One of the carvings in this book, for example, was made of a new friend who helped my husband and me when our trailer was "totaled" by a truck as we were stopped by the side of the road. A. Charles (Chuck) Artinian allowed us to stay at his ARA Motel with our dogs (normally not allowed), then lifted our low spirits at his Corn Crib restaurant with his wonderful personality, great staff, and fun atmosphere. If you are ever in Gap, Pennsylvania, I recommend that you stop in and say "hi," have a great meal, and tell him Mary Finn sent you.

Egg people can be either "big headed" or more regularly proportioned—the choice is yours. Similarly, your egg can be a "whole" person or a three-quarters, legless person. It's fine to go for whatever effect or style appeals to you or what will work best with your subject. There are no rules and nothing is set in stone! The important thing is to have fun and experiment with different looks.

Start with an idea. Draw a basic picture of your idea but don't feel that you are stuck with either the drawing or idea. Let your imagination go! Sometimes I will start to make one egg person only to end up with something completely different when the carving is done.

Get ideas by "looking" at friends and family, by observing at work, at school, in magazines, on TV, anywhere you find people. It sometimes helps to start with a profession, job, or activity, such as a hockey player, plumber, doctor, construction worker, etc. Other great sources of ideas can be computer graphics books (such as the one that catalogues your graphic library), coloring books (they have simple drawings that often work out very well), children's books, even the Internet.

Once you decide on who or what you want to carve, let your mind go—what characteristics or items do you associate with this person? Try to get these ideas on paper either by listing or drawing them. I often start with the outline of an egg and then try to see how the person would "fit" in the egg. Draw the egg shape with a marker or indelible pen so that you can erase the other marks as you need to.

Sometimes it can be helpful to start the drawing with a tool or characteristic that the person will hold or have with them, then draw or form the person around it. Do whatever works for you, since you are the one doing the project. It doesn't matter that I do it one way— you are you, so do your own thing!

Don't worry if you can't draw. This preliminary drawing is just for you—no one else has to see it. Just put down the lines, outlines, and plans you have. The drawing will help you better visualize what your egg person will look like, and if you don't like what you see you can make adjustments before you even start. Think about what wood needs to be removed, where the arms, head, and other parts will "fit" in, and so on. The drawing should also help you determine if your idea will work or not— whether it is too complex or too simple. Sometimes it is helpful to leave the drawing for a while and come back to it after a period of time. Coming back with a "fresh" look can often resolve any misgivings or problem areas.

To illustrate the various steps in this book I've used multiple eggs at different stages of carving—similar to a classroom setting. This also helps you see that each egg can have its own individual personality. I recommend that you begin with the Santa carving, as each successive project represents a slightly more challenging project. Where the steps for carving are the same as in a previous project (facial features, for example), I'll refer you back to the more detailed description provided earlier.

One important consideration before we go any further: where do you find and purchase eggs? I have found many great sources for eggs in mail order woodcarving catalogues and on the Internet. If you have problems finding wooden eggs, please feel free to contact me and I will give you some leads. You can contact me through Schiffer Publishing or e-mail me at marycfinn@email.com. I also have some ideas on my homepage: http://home.earthlink.net/~smzmfinn.

Now it is time to get started . . .

Tools

Tools are very important to the carver. One's tools must be sharp and well maintained. Each carver has his or her own favorite tools—shown here are the ones I've used in this book. I consider them like a member of my family as I spend a lot of time with them! You do not have to have the exact same tool; something similar that you feel comfortable with will work.

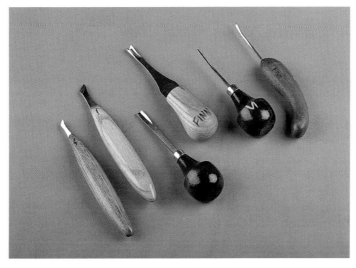

First I have The Tool Family. Shown from left to right are a small skew, medium skew, large U-gouge, large V-tool, small V-tool, even smaller V-tool.

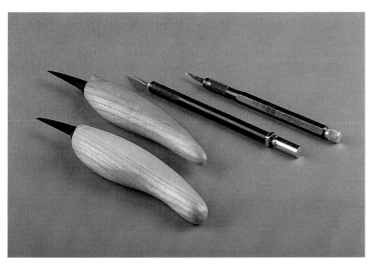

Next is the Knife Family, which includes the tools I probably use the most. On the left are two detail knives of slightly different shape; on the right are two X-Acto™ knives with different handles and blades.

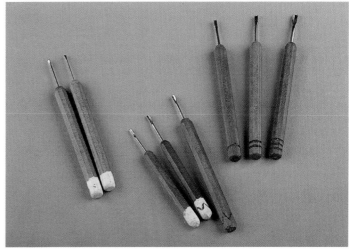

Last but by no means least I have The Micro Family, which I could not be without. Shown are skews, a variety of V-tools, and U-gouges.

Project One:
Santa Claus

Before you begin, you must orientate your egg. This ensures that the grain of the egg will not pop away as you carve, causing you to lose small features such as the nose. As you can see, I have used a pen to highlight the grain line for you. You want your face to be where the long grain lines are (see arrows), so the grain runs through the face. You do not want to carve where you can see the circles.

Start by drawing the brim—make a line that is high in the front (so you have lots of room for the face) and lower in the back, being sure to leave room for the tassel to flop over the brim. Note that I am using a black marker in this picture. Normally I use pencil, but the marker makes it easier for you to see the lines on my egg. I recommend pencil for your project — a marker may bleed into the wood and you may have to carve too deeply to remove the lines.

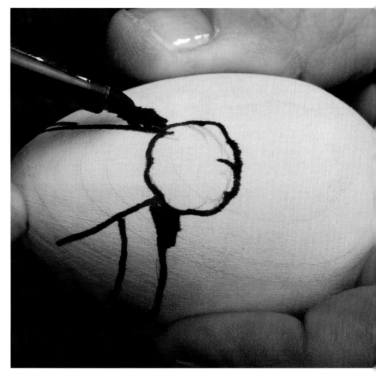

Draw the tassel, making sure it looks like the brim line continues on underneath it. You can see by the dark areas next to the tassel how the flow of the brim will go. If you need to, draw the line all the way through—you can erase it later after you get it aligned correctly.

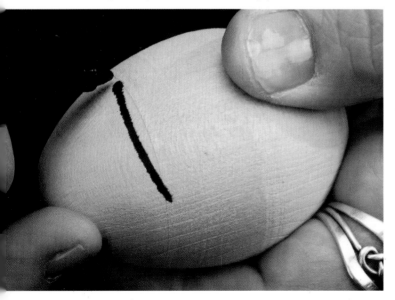

Mark a line for the bottom of the nose. The nose is the basis for the whole face, so this helps keep us on track. The nose knows! When I carve, I base everything on the nose.

Now draw in the sides of the nose, the cheeks, the mustache, the beard, a lip, and some eyes. Don't worry if you are not an expert drawer—these are just your guidelines for the carving to follow.

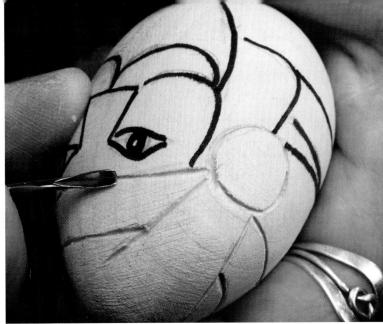

V-cut all the lines of the hat, then stop cut the same lines. The reason we V-cut the lines before stop cutting is for accuracy. You can take shorter, more accurate cuts with the V-tool, making a track to put your knife in when you stop cut. That way, even if you lose the drawn line, your cut will be deeper, providing you with a reference point.

Hair, arm, and belt are next. The hair is created by an arced line that starts at the side of the face (approximately where the mustache is), then goes around the egg and ends up in the same place on the opposite side. The arm is simply a right angle with a tiny triangle colored in to make the elbow. The belt is formed by two parallel lines: the lower one lines up approximately with the lower part of the arm and the upper one is drawn above it depending on how thick you want the belt to be. Now we are ready to carve.

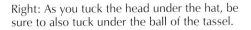

Right: As you tuck the head under the hat, be sure to also tuck under the ball of the tassel.

Before you begin working on the hat, tuck the head underneath it. This will ensure that Santa's hat fits his head properly.

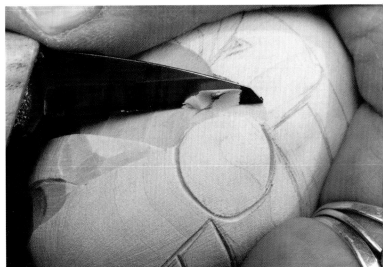

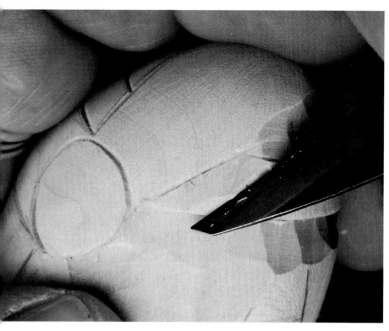

Tuck the hat and the brim under the tassel.

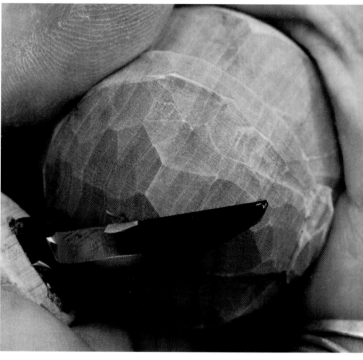

Round the top of the head, making it all nice and smooth.

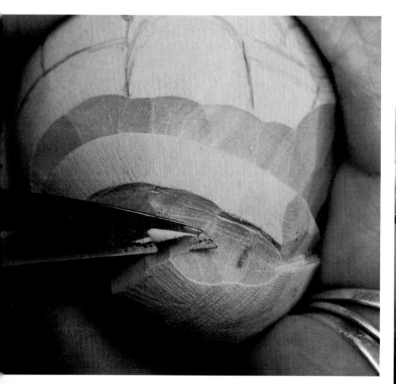

Taper the hat so that it is lower than the brim.

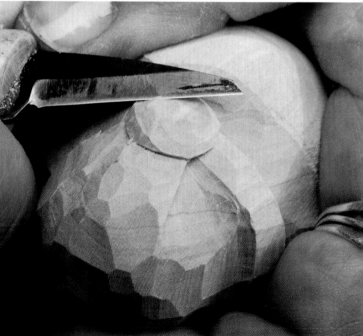

Finish the hat by smoothing the brim and rounding the tassel and ball. It doesn't have to be completely finished at this stage—just "in the ball park."

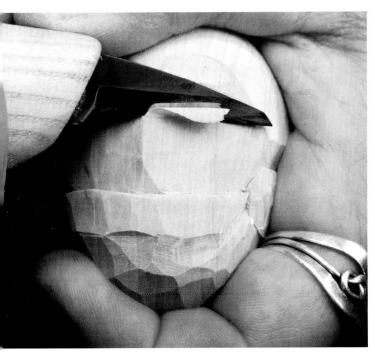

Slope and taper the face so that the area in the center of the face is the highest, sloping towards the side of the face. This will make the nose extend forward and out from the face. This sloping and tapering starts to create the triangulation of the nose.

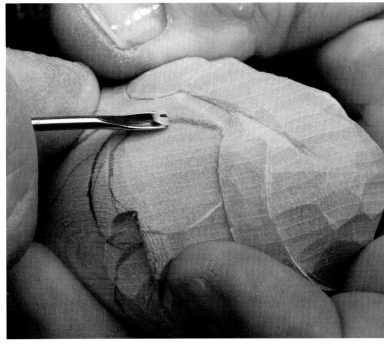

Now we're ready to start the face. V-cut the outline of the face, but don't do the sides of the nose or the eyes yet. We are only doing the outline of the face at this point.

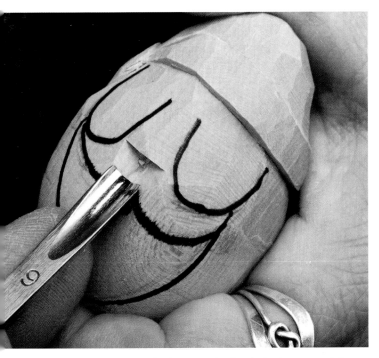

If you need to, redraw the lines. To further help the nose stick out from the face, make a stop cut on the line that you drew for the bottom of the nose. Then use a full size U-gouge to remove the wood under the bottom of the nose and taper up toward the stop cut. You may need to repeat your stop cuts and U-gouges in order to get the depth desired.

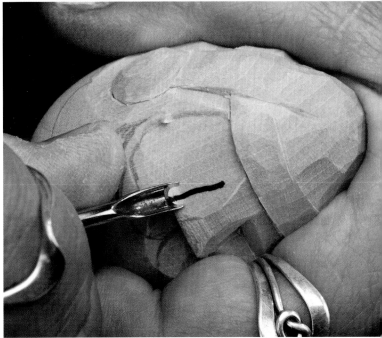

U-gouge up the sides of the nose with a micro U-gouge. This will further define the nose and help separate it from the face. We use a U-gouge so that the sides of the nose are soft, just like a real nose—no sharp lines separate the nose from the face.

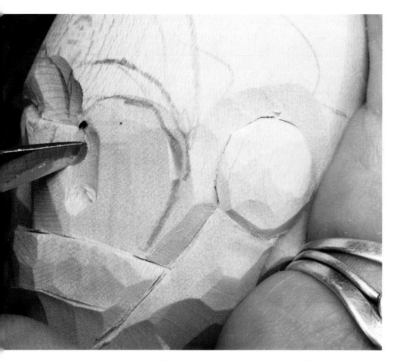

To start shaping the sides of the nose, use your knife to carve up towards the top of the nose. Be sure the tip of your knife does not dig into the cheek/face, as a nose blends into and is a part of the face, not something separate from or added to the face.

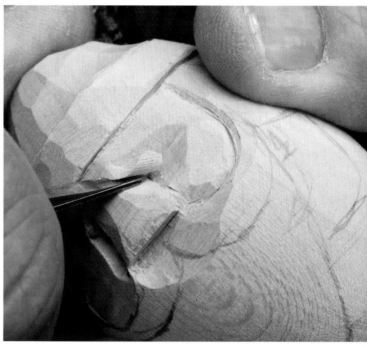

Now come back and do a little more tapering on the nose. The nose should be smooth and blend into the face and eye socket. The eye socket should be nice and clean at this point and also flow from the cheeks.

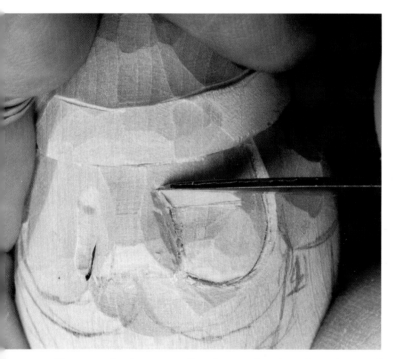

The eye socket is next. We'll make one slice down from the top of the nose and another coming from the cheek, forming a "trough" for the eye socket. If needed, do additional slices until you reach your desired depth and/or shape.

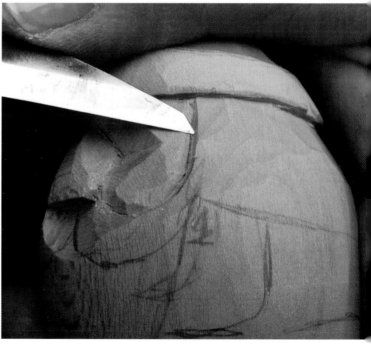

Stop cut in the outline of the face that you V-cut earlier. Taper the edges of the face into this cut to start the rounding of the face. Complete the rounding process by smoothing and tapering all areas of the face.

Here's what your Santa should look like at this point.

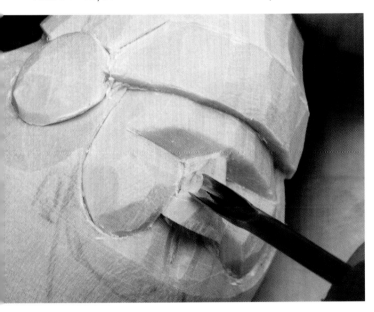

We'll begin shaping the nose by making what I like to call the "orbs," or the "balloony" part of the nose. Take a micro U-gouge and dig straight in, perpendicular to the nose, approximately one-third up from the bottom of the nose. The gouge in this picture is pointing to the spot where you should cut. It does not show the angle of the cut.

I have colored in the area above the U-gouge. That's the part we will now remove to further shape the nose.

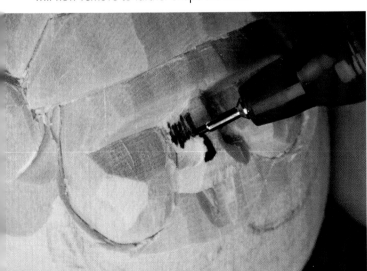

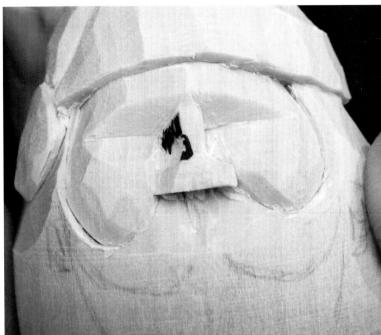

In this picture, the right side has been carved (tapered and shaped), while the left still shows the colored area for comparison.

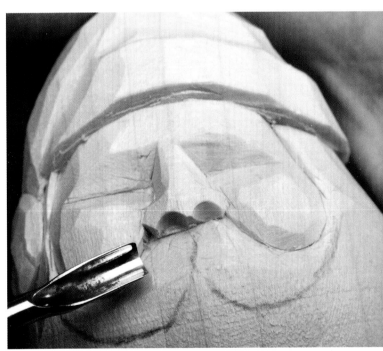

U-gouge the bottom of the nose to make the nostrils, so Santa can breathe. Notice that I have also cut a tiny triangle at the very outside edge of both sides of the nose. This gives the nose further shape and realism. I've also checked and adjusted the tucking of the cheeks and face, making improvements as needed.

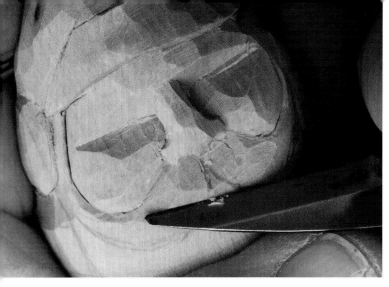

We're ready to begin Santa's mustache. Make sure the area under the nose is rounded and smoothed before starting this step.

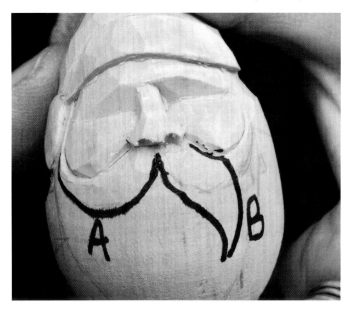

First, redraw the mustache. It can be either an up mustache or a down mustache. In this picture, A shows the up look, B shows the down look. Go for the look you like— just make both sides the same! For the purpose of this carving, Santa's mustache will be an "uppy."

V-cut and then stop cut the mustache lines.

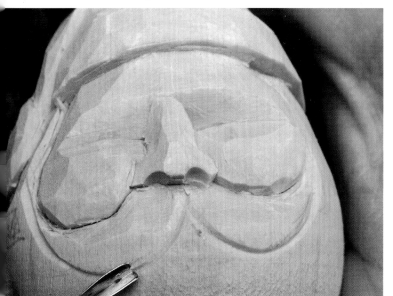

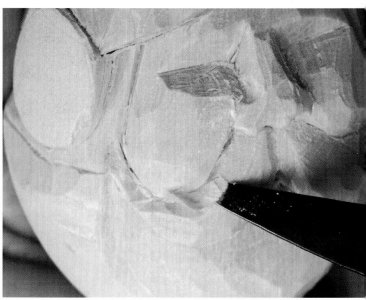

Round the mustache. Don't be afraid to dig in by the face to make those cheeks nice and chubby!

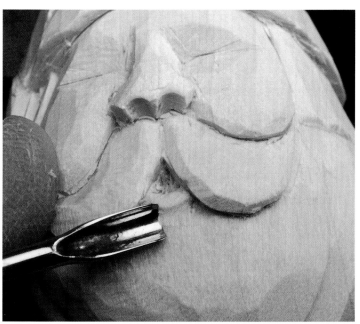

To make the mouth, cut out a triangular opening at the middle of the mustache. Then gouge a little ways under that with a micro U-gouge to form the lip. Feather the bottom edge of the U-gouge into the beard—this makes the lip stand out.

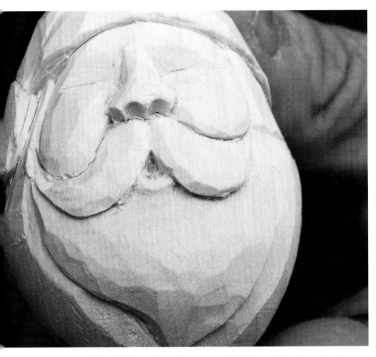

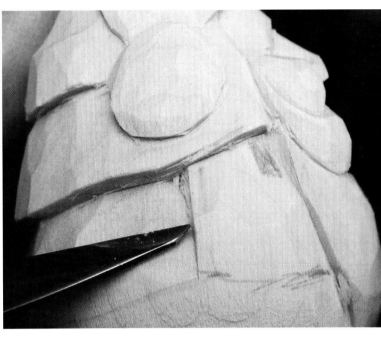

For Santa's beard, first V and stop cut the line of the beard, then slightly lower the adjacent area so the beard will stand out. Round and shape the beard.

Taper the body under the hair, so that the hair sticks out more than the body. This is done using a slice cut all the way around. We won't do any more with the hair for now, though if you have any "flyaway" hairs, gently slice them away. No gel needed for control . . . !

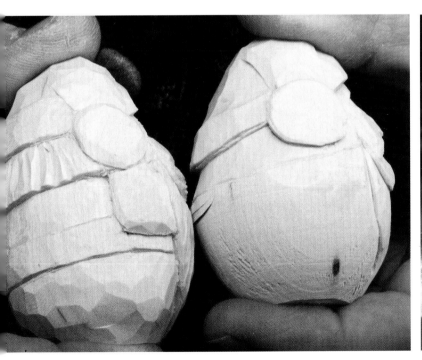

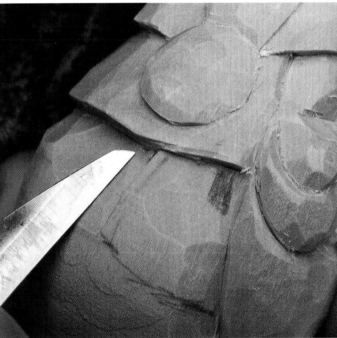

Next we will set up the hair area. To help you see where we're going, I'm holding a finished egg on the left, while the one in process is on the right. Start by V-cutting and then stop cutting the line of the hair.

Here I am starting Santa's arms. As usual, V-cut and stop cut first. Then lower the body under the arm, both along the side and underneath the arm.

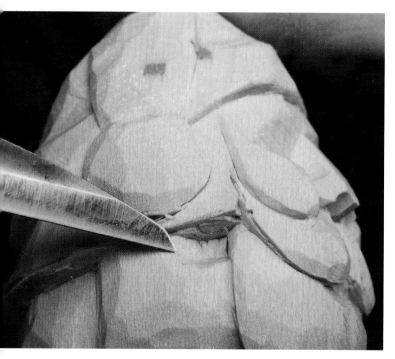

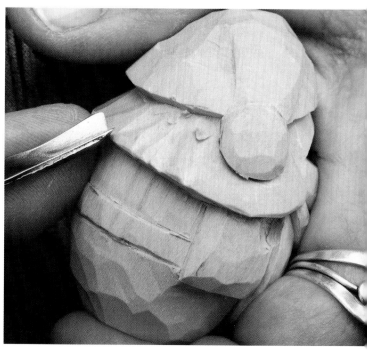

Time to make a little opening so the arm has some bend to it—if you recall, this was the colored in area from the original drawing. Start with a V-cut and stop cut, then use a combination of knives and gouges (whatever works best for you) to clean out this area. Now go ahead and shape the arm by rounding and smoothing it.

Time to add some details. Let's begin with the hair, since it is least likely to be damaged while we complete the other, more fragile, details. Start with a good size V-tool (usually from a standard set, rather then the micros) and V up towards the hat brim, making sure you don't damage it. Do this all around the head. Use a variety of cut paths to reach the top. Have some cuts that only go part way or begin other than at the edge. Not all hairs are the same.

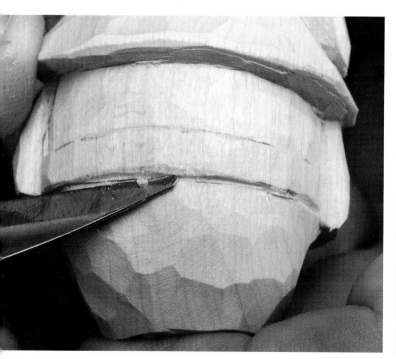

Santa's belt is the next item on our agenda. As before, start by V-cutting and stop cutting the lines. Then taper the back and the lower back under the belt so the belt is higher, just like in real life. Now go ahead and shape the belt as desired.

Next, come back with a smaller micro V, which will add flow and character to the hair. Again, use a variety of lengths for interest and reality. Don't make all your cuts straight in—give them flow, as you would find in normal hair. The smaller V-cuts provide greater detail, accenting the wider cut of the larger V. If your cuts are not coming clean at the brim of the hat, just redo your stop cut and they will pop out nicely.

To finish the hair, turn Santa on his head and use your large V-tool to carve the underside of the hair.

Now to begin the eyes. First draw the outlines, if you've lost them while doing your other steps. Then, using your micro V-tool, cut the eye outline. Start first at the center and work towards the outside corner, then start from the middle and go towards the other corner. Don't try to make the cut in one fell swoop (going from corner to corner), as you are likely to go flying off into never-never land! Once you've established a track for yourself with the initial V-cuts, you can go back over the cuts in one continuous motion to make the line of the cut smooth and even. Do the same for the other eye.

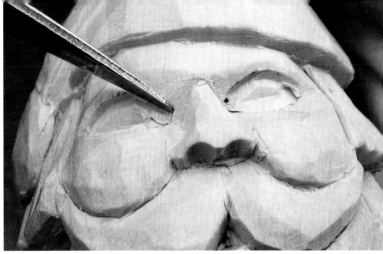

Next, stop cut in your V-cut line. You can now start from one corner and go across, as you've already established a track. You don't need to go very deep.

We are now going to remove a small triangular area in each corner of the eye. It should be deepest in the corner, sloping towards the middle of the eye. You can see one of the triangles to be removed in the outer corner of the eye on the right.

In this picture, I have completed the last step described on the left side only. You can see that it is starting to make the eyeball look more rounded, as opposed to lying flat.

Now tuck the edges of the eyeball under the eyelids, both on the top and the bottom. This will begin to round the eyes some more. The right side is still untouched, for comparison.

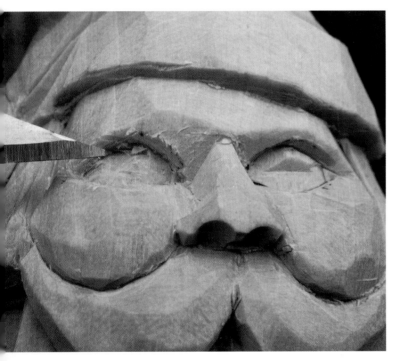

Continue rounding the eyeball until it is smooth and even all over. Don't worry if you don't get the entire crease out of the center of the eye—this doesn't show in the final carving. Our final Santa has been left with some center crease in his eye to show this. I often use an X-Acto™ knife at this point since it has such a fine, thin blade and allows me to remove very small controlled pieces as needed for the perfect look. Notice that the eye looks a bit sunken at this point. However . . .

. . . we can fix the sunken look by lowering the edges of the eye. Slice upwards on the cheek towards the eye until you have a more natural appearance. You can do the same thing on the upper eyelid as needed. For the final step, extend the V-cut/stop cut of the upper eyelid past the normal edge into the face. Then tuck the area under this cut so that the wood here is under or lower than the cut. This makes the eye appear larger and more natural.

The eye should look like this when you have completed these steps. (The eye on the left side is complete while the one on the right is at the beginning of this step for comparison). Go ahead and complete the same steps on the other eye.

To add character to the face, give Santa some "bags." Using your micro V-tool, cut two arched lines under the eye. The line closest to the eye runs from the nose to approximately two-thirds the length of the eye. The second line should be slightly shorter, maybe only half way.

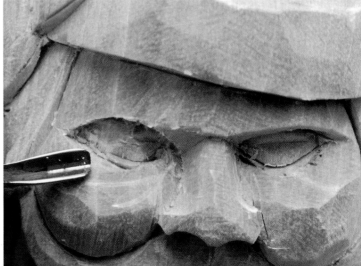

Turn Santa around so that his bottom end is toward your face. Using your micro V-tool, cut the lines of the eyebrows. Remember that a little bit of an arc is better than straight lines. Sometimes one eye side works best if you start from the eye and work out, while the other side chips and must be worked from the tip of the brow hair towards the eye. Do whatever works best.

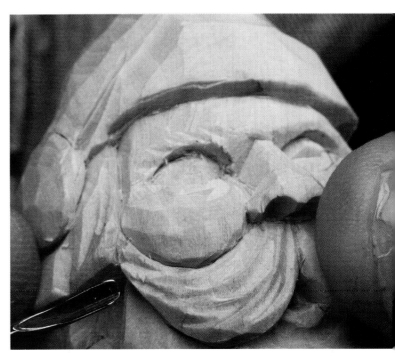

Now come back with the smaller micro V-tool and make smaller cuts, filling in the empty spaces. This gives more definition and interest to the mustache.

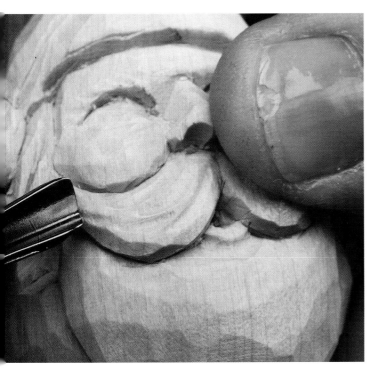

Let's add some detail to the mustache. Start with your larger V-tool and make hair cuts following the flow of the mustache. Make a number of cuts of varying lengths. Don't worry about filling in the whole area—we are just establishing highs and lows at this point. If you aren't happy with the result, just shave it a little and start again.

We are finally ready for the beard. The technique used is the same as for the hair and mustache: start with the larger V-tool to add height and definition, coming back with the smaller V to give detail, depth, and interest. Remember not to make straight lines, and use a variety of lengths and depths so the beard looks more interesting and natural. This picture shows what you are aiming for.

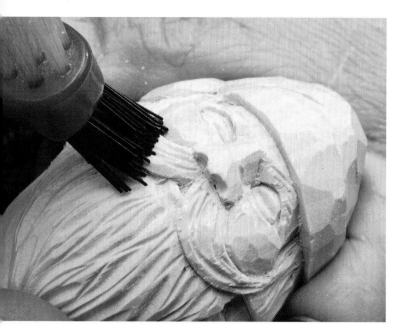

I use a denture brush to go over Santa and get rid of any loose particles of wood (known as "glunkies" in MaryFinn lingo). Just a note about the paint before we begin. I like more of a "wash" look than a heavy paint for my carvings. The finished project should look like it was carved in wood, not made of plastic. I use watercolors as they allow me to control the intensity of the color by the amount of water I use in relation to paint. The only exception is white. For white areas, I use an acrylic for its covering powers—white watercolor looks too washed out. Now we are ready to paint!

White comes next. Notice that I am going from the lightest colors to the darkest. I use white for the brim of the hat, the hair, the tassel, the beard, and the mustache. Go ahead and even cover the lips. When using the white, be careful not to get it on other areas, as it is very difficult to paint over. Sometimes I'll even use my knife to "erase" any excess white. In all of your painting, don't forget the undersides (for example, under the edge of the hair and under the brim of the hat).

Painting Santa begins with flesh color. I mix white, yellow, orange, and brown together—whatever it takes to get the warm hue I'm after. Often I will make a large amount of flesh so when I get a color I like I can rejuvenate it with water for future use. Remember to keep water to a minimum—too much water will raise the grain of the wood and you could lose some of the features (all that hard work for nothing). Less water also means less drying time—but a hair dryer can help in a pinch! Also, be careful how you hold your egg so that you don't pick up color on your fingers and get paint where it doesn't belong. Now go ahead and paint the whole face, even inside the eyeballs.

Red is used for Santa's clothes and hat. I mix a little orange in my red, to give it a warm, jolly, Christmas Santa hue. I also keep this color very transparent, so you can see the grain. Don't forget the bottom! If the beard is dry enough, you can also paint in Santa's red lip at this time. I use a slightly watered down red for inside the mouth and have also added a little rosiness (with a very "weak" red) to Santa's cheeks and nose.

Now I'll use black for the belt and the inside of the eye. Don't forget the edges of the belt (top and bottom). If desired, another color can be used for the eyes. Whatever color you use, be sure your brush (and the white paint already applied) are both very dry, or the colors will bleed into each other. Be aware of the water content on your brush throughout so you don't bleed onto neighboring colors. Dabbing your brush with a paper towel occasionally will help absorb some of the extra water. When you paint the inside of the eye, remember that it is not a completely round ball. If you look at your own eye, the colored part is not totally visible—part of it is hidden by the lower eyelid.

Add a tiny dot of white to each eye as a focal point. Now Santa has that famous twinkle in his eye! Finish your carving by adding a water based acrylic varnish after everything is completely dry. Be careful when applying this: even though the paint has dried, it can still bleed because we've used watercolors. It is best to do all of one color first, starting with the lightest, then clean off your brush and go on to the next. If needed, another coat may be added. For this coat, you can varnish all over as the colors have been "set" by the first coat of varnish. Let dry completely, then enjoy your Santa!

Project Two
The Man ("Dad")

For the man (Dad), first orientate your egg as you did with the Santa figure, making sure the grain will be going up and down through Dad's face. Then draw a half circle to suggest where the bottom of the chin and the sides of the face will be. I have also drawn a horizontal line going around the man's back at the level of his shoulders.

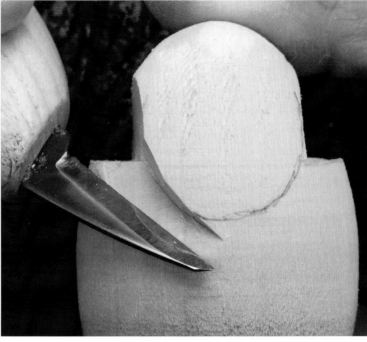

Stop cut on the line that you drew for the head. Then slice up to the stop cut from below the line. This will make the face stick out from the body. You didn't need to V-cut first because we want a straight sharp line here.

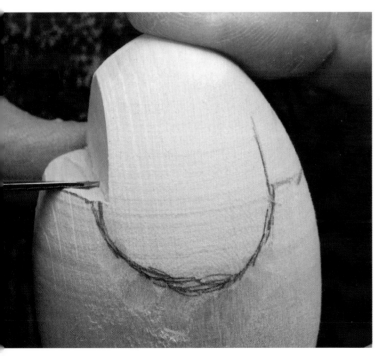

Stop cut the shoulder line, slice down to it, and remove the area from the shoulder to the head line. You will need many stop cuts and slices to accomplish this.

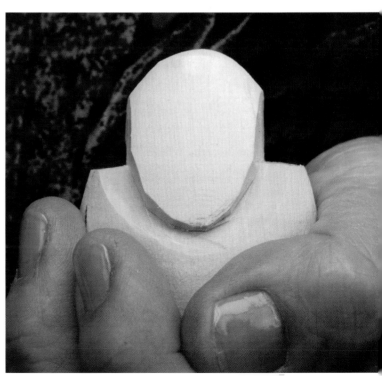

This is how your egg should look once you've done both sides.

Now draw the arm, including a downward section (upper arm), forward section (lower arm), and a rounded end where the hand will be. Just a basic outline is fine—it doesn't need to be too fancy.

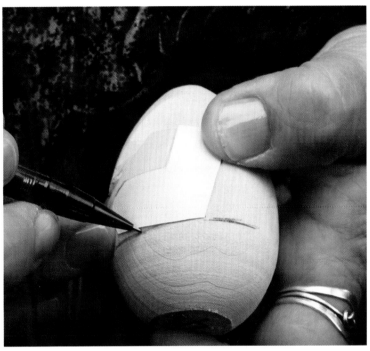

This shows how a paper template could be used to match up the other arm. You can also see the line I've drawn around the back.

I like to draw lines at the top, where the arms meet the shoulders on both sides of the head. This way I know my arms will line up and I won't have a misshapen egg person. I then draw the other arm, using the two lines at the top as reference points. If needed, you can draw another line around the back to line up the elbows. I often use my fingers as measuring sticks, to compare from side to side. Still another option is to make a paper template so the arms will be exactly the same.

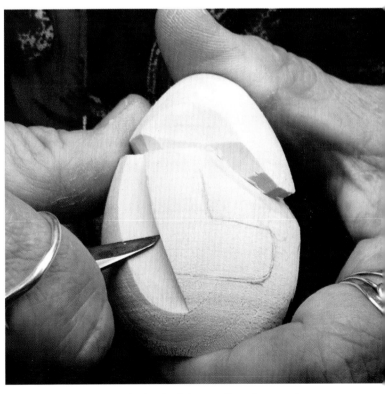

Now V-cut and stop cut the back of the arm line, then continue with stop cuts and slices to lower the wood from the backside (where the back will be) of the arm.

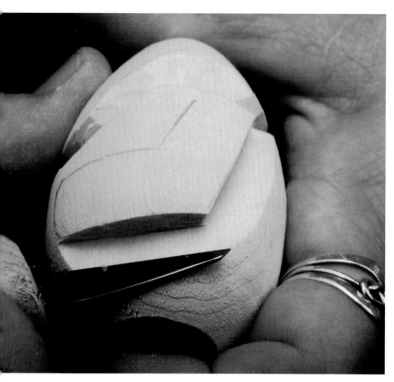

Repeat the same process for the lower arm. At this point, the back part of the arm should stick out from the rest of the body.

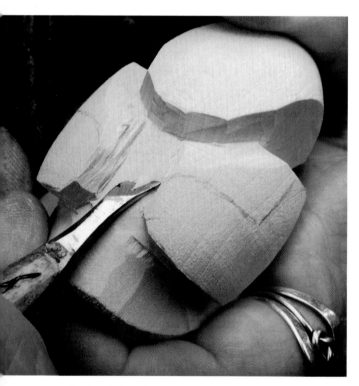

To further define the arms, remove the area between the hands using a combination of knives, gouges, and skew—whatever you feel most comfortable with.

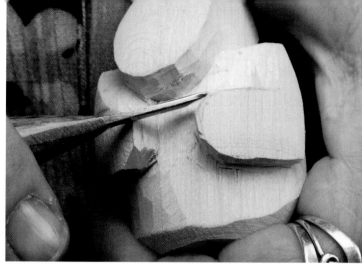

V-cut and stop cut the inside of the arm line, again using your knife, gouges, and skew. Remove this area.

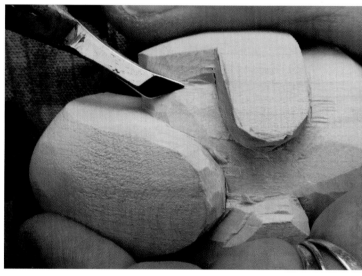

Taper the body towards the shoulders and towards the center of the egg.

The completed figure so far. Notice that we are not done shaping at this point, we are just getting things in position for the carving to come later. At this point, the area under the arms should be tapered towards the bottom of the egg and be nice and rounded.

Taper the back up and under the head. Don't worry that the back of the head appears to protrude too far at this point—we haven't shaped the head yet.

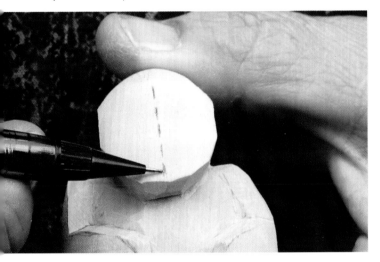

Next I like to make a little dashed line to indicate the center of the face. I use a dashed line instead of a straight line because we won't be V-cutting or stop-cutting it —it's a reference point only. The dashed line reminds me not to stop or V-cut this line.

As with Santa, we want Dad's face to peak towards our center dash line, so the nose will project out from the face and have a triangular shape. Compare the right side of the face—where I have completed this step—with the left, uncompleted side.

Draw a straight line where you want the bottom of the nose to be, then draw the two side lines.

Stop cut the line under the nose, then slice up to it from the chin to make the nose stick out from the face.

Let's do the side of the nose now. First U-gouge up to the top of the nose, as shown here on the left. Then carve the eye socket, as shown on the right (for more detail on eye sockets, see the Santa project, pages 15-16).

At this point our head looks pretty unusual, so let's round it a bit and make it look more human. Don't aim for perfection, just more of a head shape. Caution: be sure you leave enough wood so you'll be able to make the ears stick out from the rest of the head later.

Let's draw in the hairline and the outline of the ears, remembering that the forward part of the ear should line up with the center of the head.

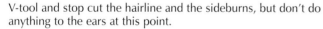

V-tool and stop cut the hairline and the sideburns, but don't do anything to the ears at this point.

Taper the face a little under the hair. This gives us the boundaries we need for completing the face. If the face is a little too fat, go ahead and taper it a bit now as well.

U-gouge a third of the distance from the bottom of the nose, going straight in and towards the face to make the orbs. Then taper the part above the U-gouge towards the bridge of the nose, giving the nose a nice realistic shape.

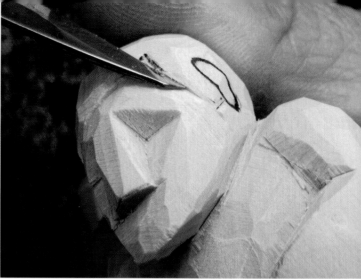

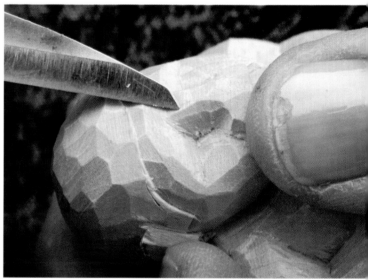

Let's give Dad some smile lines. From the bottom of the orbs (U-gouge on the side of the nose), draw a line down to the bottom of the chin at a slight angle. Stop cut this line with your knife.

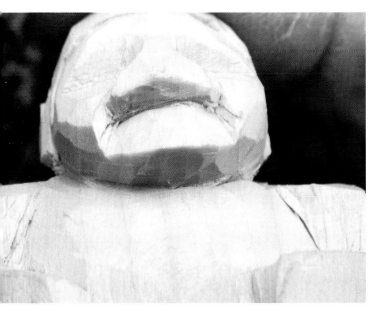

Our next step is to mound the mouth area, so that it is highest in the middle and tapered towards the smile lines on both sides of the face.

Begin removing the hard edges of the arm a little at a time, rounding towards the middle as you go. To eliminate the existing roundness of the egg shape, the arm also needs to be tapered from the elbow down towards the hand, giving it a more realistic look. In this picture, I've gone ahead and done this on the left side, as shown by the angle of my knife.

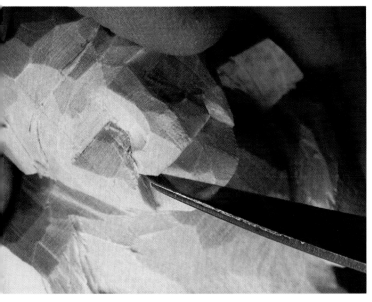

Just like in the Santa carving, remove a small triangular piece from the corner of each side of the nose. This helps round the nose, giving it more realism. We'll leave the details of the face till the end of our carving so they won't get damaged while we work on other areas.

We won't carve the complete ear just yet, but we do need to set up the area in which the ear will be carved later. V-tool and stop cut around the outline you drew earlier, then taper the head so it is lower than the ear. We'll finish the detailing of the ear later.

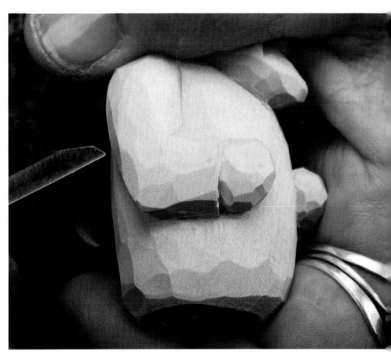

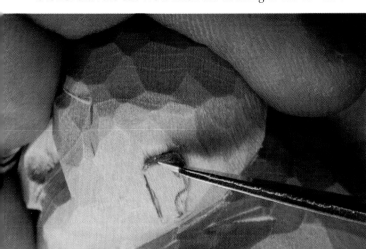

Don't worry about separating the hand from the arm until everything is more or less rounded. And don't hesitate to remove more wood from under the arms or on the back, if the arm is not sticking out enough.

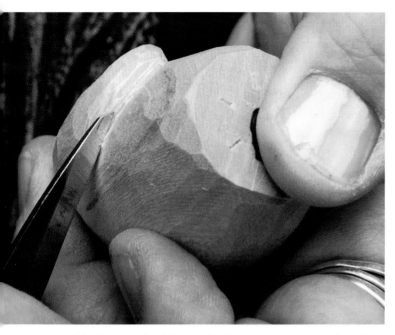

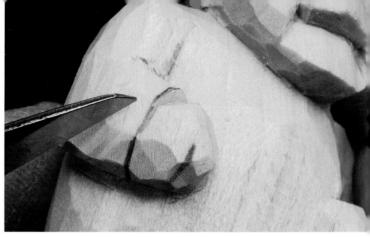

Draw the line where you want the hand to be in relationship to the arm. Then stop cut the line.

To help the outside of the arm look even more separate from the body, I make a V-slice to form what I like to call a magic triangle* into the area where the arm touches the body. This helps the arm look more rounded and separate from the body. Especially emphasize the V-cut (magic triangle) at the elbow.

>*called a magic triangle because of how "like magic" the triangular cut better defines and separates what you are working on.

Continue separating and shaping the hand. Use your "magic triangle" at the upper and lower part of the hand where it meets the sleeve to help give a roundness to the hand . We'll put the fingers in as part of the detailing later.

Now shape the back so it tapers up towards the head and has a nice form to it—not too fat and not too skinny. Dad is going to be wearing a suit jacket, so you need to be sure the whole jacket area is nice and smooth. You won't be able to correctly add the jacket details later if it's not.

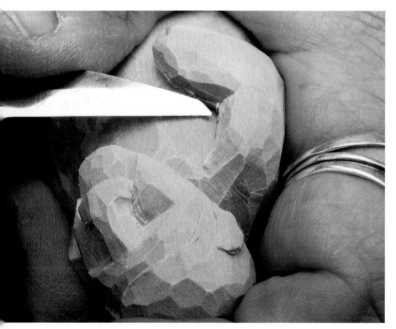

Be sure you have enough "meat" or thickness to the arms, making them both nice and rounded. The body above the arm should taper up towards the head.

Draw in the jacket and tie. The jacket includes the lapels, pockets, and the bottom edge of the jacket. At this point you may want to flatten the bottom of the egg to give it a nice flat surface.

Stop cut in the tie lines and the outside edge of the jacket. You can also remove the area on the side of the tie by the knot. Here it has been colored in on the left side and actually removed on the right side.

V-gouge all the lines for the jacket and tie. Don't stop cut them all now, however—wait until you are ready to work on each one individually (V-cutting all the lines first saves time and prevents you from losing a line while working on another part).

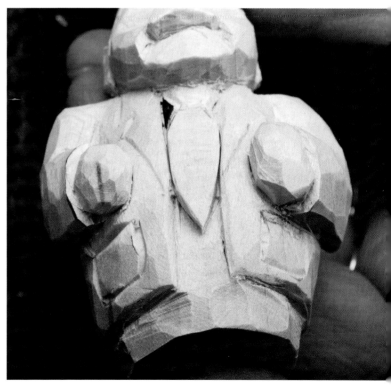

Now lower the area under the bottom of the tie so that the tie becomes slightly higher. At this time you can also stop cut and lower the area under the jacket.

27

Let's shape the tie by rounding the knot and tapering the edges to give it more interest. Be sure to lower the bottom part of the tie under the knot. Finish the tie by rounding and tapering it towards the point or tip.

Now for the lapels. Stop cut in the V-cut you did earlier, then slightly lower the jacket so the lapel is a bit higher. You don't want the lapel to be too high or it will look phony. A skew is very helpful for this step.

Now lower the area outside the pocket. I want this to be very gentle, so I don't even stop cut it first. If you've done a nice V-cut, you should be able to remove just one edge of the V-cut and create the outline of the pocket.

OK, we are ready for the details! Begin by drawing four little lines to separate the fingers. Then come along with a very small, fine V-tool and go over the lines. In this picture, the left side has been drawn and the right side has been cut.

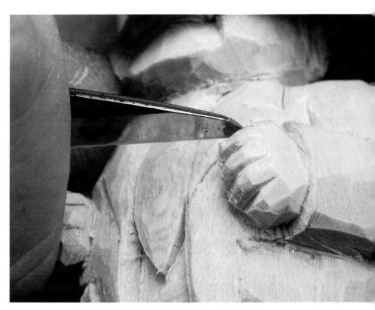

Come back with your knife and increase the V-cuts as needed to make the fingers rounder. Be sure that the thumb is shorter than the fingers! The hand and fingers should be rounded and finished now.

Next let's finish the nose—Dad certainly wants to breathe! With your U-gouge, go down and straight in to form the nostrils, then finish up any tapering or shaping that may be necessary.

To begin the eyes, draw them in the correct location, then V-cut and stop cut the line. Remember to start in the middle with your V-cut, working to the outside corners to establish your track. Don't try to go all the way across at one time until you have established the track!

To continue the eye, first make a triangle in both corners as shown in the colored area on the left side of this picture. Then tuck the eyeball underneath the eyelids and round the eyeball. Although this makes the eye look kind of sunken, we'll fix it in the next step.

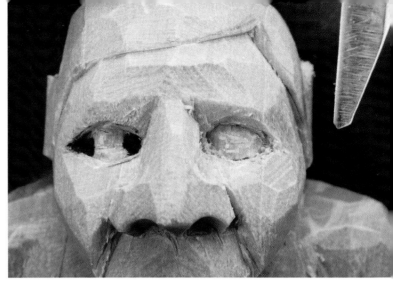

To correct the sunken eye problem, I've lowered the cheek and upper eyelid so that the eye is more lifelike. I have only worked on the right side to show more easily what I've done. Remember that the human head naturally indents a little by the eyes so that the forehead and cheek area stick out a little more on the sides. If needed, you can also taper the forehead a bit at this point to give a better shape to the brow.

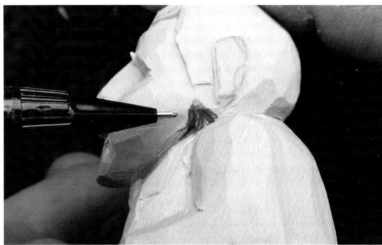

To give the jaw a more natural line, I have colored in a little triangle that separates the head from the neck. Remember the magic triangle? Go ahead and remove this little piece (magic triangle)—it doesn't have to be very deep. This will also assist in making the ear stand out more.

Here's what your man should look like with the triangle removed. Note that I removed a little wood from under the ear as well.

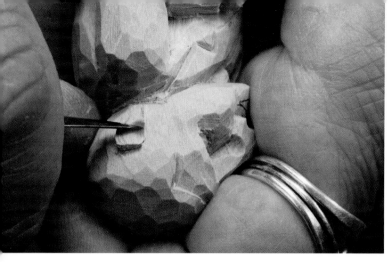

To carve the ear, we must first angle the wood reserved for the ear towards the front of the head. The outside or back edge of the ear needs to be away from the head while the front of the ear should be flush with the face.

Your ear should now look something like this. Don't go too deep or you may chip off vital parts of the ear without meaning to.

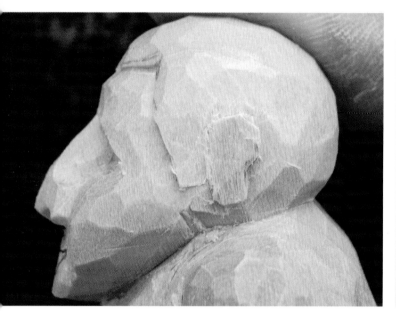

Now go ahead and give some shape to your ear. I like to put a little "hook" or curve in the back edge of the ear. Sometimes the grain won't allow this—in that case, just round it off.

Draw a line for the recessed part of the ear. It is simplified since we are working in such a small area, yet it will create a very realistic ear. Be careful not to draw too close to the edges—you don't want the ear to fall off when you start to carve it!

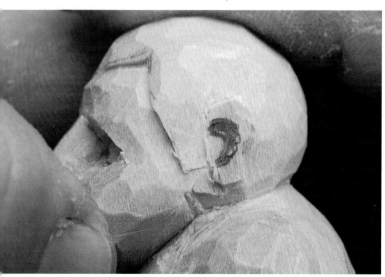

Here's an example of a more rounded ear. The grain on this egg was a little more chippy so I was afraid I might lose the ear if I made it more detailed. This simple ear still works very nicely as well.

As long as we're working on the head, let's go ahead and do the hair. First put in the part, which goes from the forehead back. Then direct the hair down towards the ear and neck area on one side of the part and across the top of the head on the other side of the part. Remember to get flow and variety in the hair by first using a large V-tool then a micro V-tool and varying the shape, length, and size of your cuts.

Now, since Dad is such a happy guy, we are going to create a nice big smile on his face. You can see that I begin by drawing the pattern . . .

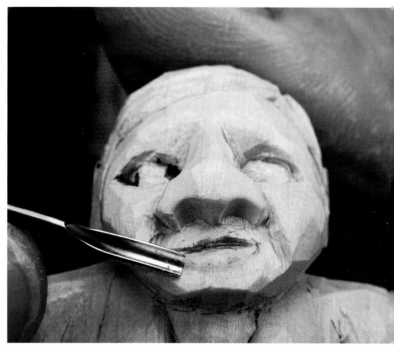

For this next step be sure you have a very sharp U-gouge that will cut cleanly any way the grain goes. I am using my micro U-gouge so that the outer edge of the tool just barely touches and removes the line of the lower lip. Notice that my tool is NOT centered on the line—just the upper edge is touching it. By the way, we are making a close mouthed Dad (not a common sight!).

. . . then I carve the upper lip using my V-tool. I do this by angling or tilting my V-tool so that the upper edge of the V-tool digs into the wood, forming a flat plane for the upper lip.

Tidying up the mouth comes next. I feather in the bottom of the U-gouge marks and round the chin a bit more as needed. I also make a stop cut in the center of the mouth, taking out a very small slice to slightly separate the lips. Additionally, I elongate the corners of the mouth, making it look slightly more realistic.

Next I can soften the smile line and taper the cheeks as needed. I'll also make a scooping type cut to form the natural curvature of the cheek towards the chin. In this picture, the right side has been completed, while the left side is the same as in the previous picture.

There is one final step to complete the mouth—we need to make the little indentation under the nose (what I fondly refer to as the "ST", or snot tunnel . . .) This will also give a little added shape to the upper lip. Start with your U-gouge on the very tip of the center of the upper lip and go straight up to between the two nostrils. The area to be gouged is colored in orange in this picture. Notice that it is not too deep, just a shallow indentation.

Below: Now give Dad any finishing touches you like, then you are ready to paint. We'll will use our chubby, open mouth model to talk about the painting (refer to the Santa carving for more details, if needed). I start with all the flesh colors first, painting the entire face area including inside the mouth, inside the eyes, the ears, and the hands. Then I paint the hair and eyebrows, being careful to wait until the face is completely dry. Next the complete eyeball is painted white, as are the teeth. Since Dad wouldn't be caught dead in lipstick, use a little brownish red hue to give a natural color to his lips. Don't forget to paint the area between the teeth —do this in a dark shade. Next come the clothes. I gave this model a blue suit, red tie, and gold tie clasp, but of course you can use any colors you like. For the finishing touches, I paint a black dot for the eyeball and a tiny white dot for a highlight. (Of course, you can give Dad brown or blue eyes, if desired!) Let dry completely, then finish so Dad will have a nice long life!

You can also carve an open mouth Dad, as seen here in the model on the left. The steps are basically the same, except of course you would draw the mouth a lot larger with an open area between the lips. V-tool and U-gouge the top and bottom lips as before, then slightly lower the middle area from the lips. Make sure the area is domed—highest in the middle and some-what lower on either side. Then draw lines for the top and bottom teeth, remembering that they should slightly arc so the teeth in the front are the biggest; those in the back, slightly smaller. U-gouge the area between the teeth, so it appears to recess back into the mouth. Individual teeth are made with a very fine V-cut to separate the teeth.

Project Three
The Butterfly Lady

To begin the butterfly lady, first make sure the grain of your egg is correct, as with the previous two projects. The grain lines should be running up and down the front of the egg, where the face will end up. Now start by drawing a line all the way around for the bottom of the hat brim. It should be a little higher in the front and a little lower in the back, just as if you were wearing a hat yourself.

Next draw a line all the way around the hat for the upper edge of the brim. Don't make it too narrow or you will lose the edges for sure and end up with a crazy looking hat!

Stop cut on the line and slice up to it, lowering the face and hair area quite a bit under the big brimmed hat (the deeper the cut, the wider the brim will end up being).

Using a scooping cut, start carving at the newly drawn line up towards the top of the head. This starts giving the hat a domed shape. Do this all the way around.

Shape the top of the hat, removing all saw marks. Don't worry if the edge of the brim is not as narrow as you might like. For safety you want it to be thick for now. We'll smooth and refine it later, but we don't want to risk losing it now.

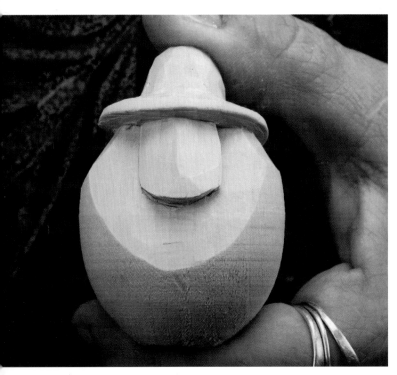

Now lower the wood around the face, then establish the ridged area for the nose. To do this, draw a dotted center reference line, then slice so the center is higher than the edges. It should look like this when you're done.

I've gone ahead and put in the facial features here. I know this is a big jump, but the steps are exactly the same as those used in the "Dad" project. Refer to those instructions as needed. The face may look a little rough and "witchy" here, but we're just establishing a basic outline for our butterfly lady. Note that I have also drawn a line for the hair all the way around the egg.

Begin working on the hair, first separating the head from the body by slicing up to and down towards the line. It may be helpful to do a V-cut, then a stop cut, then your slices. Whatever works best for you is fine. This step should not be done in one cut—a number of small cuts is safer. Go for your comfort level, but avoid having the butterfly lady wear your blood!

Time to start bringing the butterfly lady out of the egg! I begin by flattening the back area, but I don't go as far as I will ultimately end up. I want to leave myself some room to put the arms in and still have a curve to the back.

Now I have drawn on the arms. One side is curved . . .

. . . .and the other straight.

This picture shows the next several steps combined (for more detail on these steps, refer to my descriptions for the Dad egg, since the process is the same). On the left side, I have stop cut and sliced down so the arm stands out from the body, leaving it very squarish at this point. On the right side, I have started to round the arm as well as the back. I've even added a "magic triangle" to further separate the arm from the body.

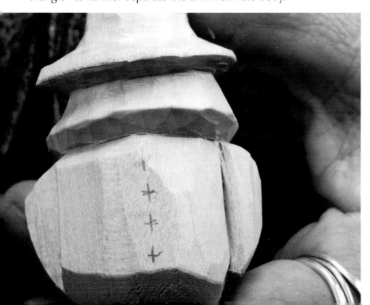

Carve the front just like you did the back. Round the body as well.

Go ahead and draw in the clothes, then V-cut all your lines. You can wait to stop cut until you are ready to complete each area.

Here I have stop cut the collar lines and lowered the shirt a little bit, so the collar will stand out slightly. And, since this is our first lady egg, we need to add her distinctive qualities. I've done this on the right side only, so you can see the difference.

The hat is really bothering me: the top is too high and the brim is too thick. We purposely left the brim thick earlier, but now it's time to fix that. I want the hat to look sort of like a safari hat, the kind a butterfly collector might wear, so I'll shorten the top of the hat and then round it. When working on the brim, try to work on the top side only as you are less likely to damage it that way. Remember, I have completed these steps on the right side only.

Since the butterfly lady is wearing a short sleeve shirt, her arm will be done a bit differently (in the Dad carving, we were able to use the jacket sleeve to separate the hand from the arm). First I establish the shirt by making a stop cut and tapering the arm under the sleeve. To make the separation between the arm and the hand, I start by going horizontally across at the wrist with a micro U-gouge. I then taper the marks of the U-gouge into the arm and the hand. You can add fingers if you like, but lots of times I leave my egg people fingerless—after all, they are caricatures.

Let's do the hair next. As usual, use two sizes of gouges to make a variety of heights, angles, and curves. This will make the hair look more natural and interesting.

For the eye details, first draw the outline of the eye, then V-cut the line starting from the center and working out to both edges. Stop cut in your V-cut, then remove the "magic triangle" in both corners (depending on the size of the eye you may skip part of these steps, even to the point of painting the eye on rather than carving it). Go with what works best for you.

Let's finish tidying up the clothes. Notice that for the rest of these pictures we'll maintain the present stage on the left side and show each new step completed on the right. This way you can see where you are and where you need to go.

Now go ahead and taper the cheek if needed, add bags under the eyes with V-cuts (one or two depending on how much room is available), and even give her some eyebrows. I've drawn the eyebrow and the bags on the left so you can see what we are aiming for.

U-gouge for the bottom lip as done in the Dad carving. Then feather the bottom of the U-gouge's edge to flow into the chin, separating the chin from the lower lip. You can soften the cheeks on the sides or leave them craggy if you prefer — it's OK either way. I've also added a little indentation between the cheek and the jaw. To make it easier to see the difference here, I've drawn a line down the middle of the chin.

On to the mouth. We will give her a happy, closed mouth so there is no chance of swallowing the butterfly! First V-cut the upper lip, especially leaning into the area just above the mouth to get a nice flat plane. Don't worry if you have difficulty getting the exaggerated plane for the upper lip; come back with your knife if you need to. Remember to add the little indentation under the nose, which gives the Cupid's bow to the lips.

Uh, oh, we almost forgot the nostrils. Use your U-gouge to go straight in, just like the others. Don't forget the "magic triangle" in the corners. Be careful, it's very small on this face.

Here is a finished butterfly lady with a slightly different look to her mouth. Notice that I've cleaned off the very flat edge of the hat brim. We want that to be very smooth and clean — otherwise when we paint, the original saw marks will absorb the paint differently.

To make the net, start by drawing the outline on a 1/8" thick piece of basswood, which can be purchased at most hobby shops. Before you cut the net out, hollow out the opening of the net for more interest and reality. I generally use a U-gouge to accomplish this. Now cut the net out using a scroll saw, band saw, or a little coping saw—whichever you feel the most comfortable and safest with is fine.

The butterfly was made out of a chip from your carving. I found one that I could see a butterfly in, drew the outline, and very carefully cut it out with an X-Acto™ knife. I placed it on a soft piece of wood (maybe a scrap left over from cutting out the net), so I would be less likely to tear it. Then I went ahead and painted the background color (a marker is often the easiest to use) and put a coat of super glue on it to give it strength and durability. I set it to the side until I was ready to glue it on.

I've gone ahead and painted the butterfly lady, starting with the face, then the white of her eye, the hair, the hat, and the body. I painted the net before I put it on. I left the net itself *au natural* and drew the lines on with a fine line permanent marker (mine did smear a little with the finish so be sure and test it ahead of time). I painted the handle a brownish color and slightly darkened the opening of the net with a bit of yellow. I did not put lines inside to further suggest an opening, though in reality you would see the back side of the net. Lastly, I took the butterfly that I made earlier, cut it in half, glued both halves at an appropriate angle, let it dry, then added the dots and body markings of the butterfly.

The Hockey Player

From this top view, you can see that I've removed the front and back colored in areas to form more or less a square. If it's a little bit rectangular, that's OK too.

Since I'm from Michigan and a huge ice hockey fan, I had to include a hockey player! With this carving I will also show you a slightly different way of setting up a head. You'll then be able to take the technique you like the best and make it your own. To start the hockey player, I drew a line completely around the egg, approximately one third of the way down (where the shoulders will be). Then I drew an arc on each side and colored in this area, leaving a space equal to the approximate width of the head. Remember to keep the grain running up and down where the nose will be. This guy has already lost some teeth — we don't want to lose the nose as well!

Now remove the four corners of the square.

Start rounding this area by tapering up towards the top. Don't try to go all the way up to the top with a single stroke or you are likely to remove more than you want. As you can see here, I do it in several stages.

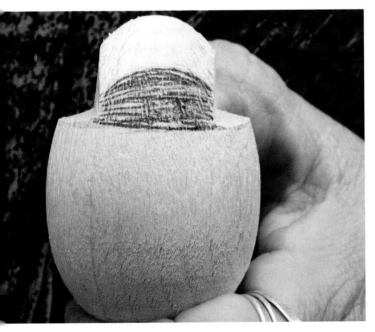

Next, remove the two colored in areas and color in a similar area at the front and back of the egg.

Go ahead and round or dome the head, making it rather smooth. At this point you can't tell front from back.

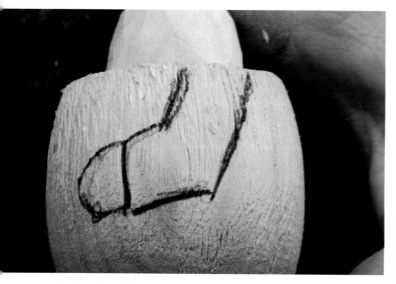

Go ahead and draw your two arms. One arm is slightly higher than the other, to properly hold the hockey stick at the end. It doesn't matter which arm is higher — just depends on whether you want him to be a righty or lefty!

Be sure the shoulders are lined up. You can use a line across the back, as we did with the previous egg people, which always helps. Now let's start flattening the back. You want to leave lots of room here, because a hockey jersey is quite large with all the protective gear underneath. Plus, this little guy is going to have legs.

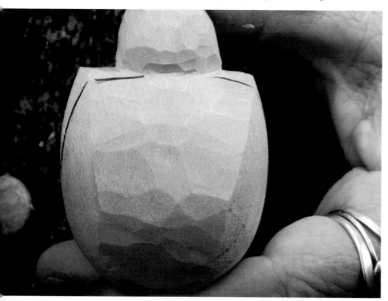

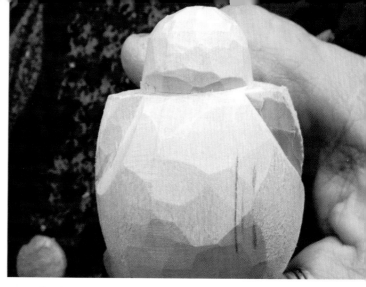

Begin the shaping by establishing the backs of the arms, so we know how much of an area we'll have to work with for the trunk and legs.

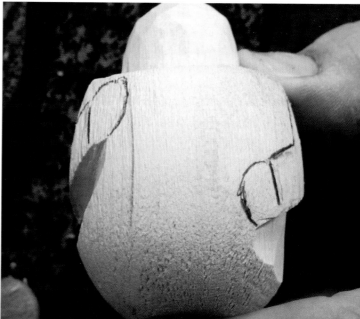

Now establish the separation of the arms from the body — we are looking at a front view here. Completing this step will allow you to know how much room you have for the trunk and legs in the front.

Go ahead and separate the area above the arm for greater definition of where everything is going to end up.

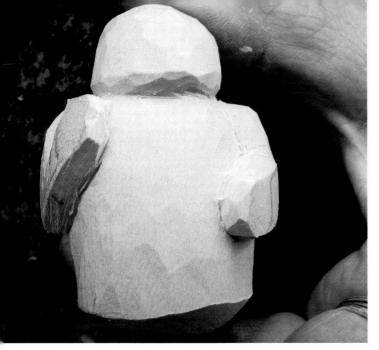

Now it's safe to go ahead and remove the middle area, pretty much shaping in an even flow down towards the bottom of the egg.

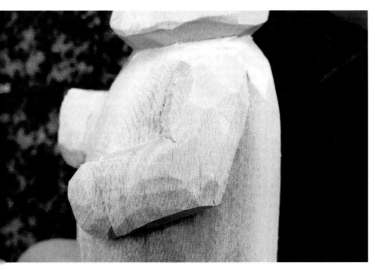

Round and shape the arms. If you need more detail on this step, refer to the previous projects.

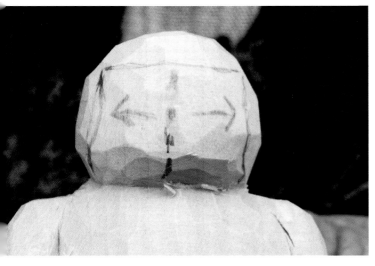

Draw the openings of the helmet and a center reference line, which will be used to establish the nose area.

Now V-cut and stop cut the helmet, then round the wood into the helmet. I've done this on the right side only so you can see the difference.

Go ahead and make a plane to help establish the nose as a triangular protuberance on the face. Do this to both sides. We'll leave the face as it is for now so we don't lose any of its fragile components during the next few steps.

For the legs and feet, first draw a line representing the bottom of the jersey. Then V-cut and stop cut on the line. If you feel comfortable enough, you can just make the stop cut but remember to use several small cuts as you go along. The right side shows what your egg should look like at this point.

Draw a line for the bottom of the shorts, then another parallel line for the top of the foot. Color in the area created by the two lines. This will help you visualize where we're going.

Refer to the steps from our previous egg people to go ahead and carve the face. You may want to give this figure a grimace so he can have his "hockey face" on. Detailing of the jersey requires just the addition of a V neck — painting will take care of the rest.

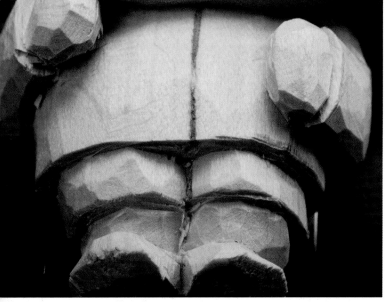

To get to this point, I made a stop cut at the bottom of the shorts then tapered the remainder slightly under the shorts. Next I created a vertical separation in the middle for the two legs, then tapered the colored in section from before down towards the skates. I will take a little bit of "poetic license" here and have this middle section represent the socks and the bottom part shaped into the skates If you prefer, you can make the whole bottom area the skates (in that case the socks would not be visible). Don't worry about the blades on the bottom of the skates: we'll be mounting our figure on a hockey puck.

Here is the front of the hockey player ready for painting . . . .

. . . and the back. Be sure and brush him off well before painting.

Here is the front of the painted hockey player. Paint as usual, starting with the flesh color for the face. Make sure you do all of the eye with the flesh as well. Next paint the jersey and socks red. Once the face is dry, mix a little brown with the red and do the lips. No hockey player would be caught dead with lipstick so make sure it is not *too* red! For humor, I added a fine red line as if he might have a healing cut. After everything was dry, I added white for the white of the eyes, the collar band, the armband stripes, the number 9 . . .

Of course, no hockey player would be complete without a stick! Take a thin piece of wood (I'm using a 1/8" piece of basswood) and line up the grain so that it is going up and down the shaft of the stick (if the grain goes across the shaft it has a tendency to break). Cut your stick out and paint it with a light coat of black watercolor (you could also make it brown, but black matches the paint job I have in mind for this hockey player). This picture show the outline for a stick plus the finished product.

. . . and on the back, my favorite player's name — Howe, for Gordie Howe! (Gordie Howe was my neighbor when I was growing up and he was wonderful to everyone. He even stopped to help one day when my bike was broken, fixed the bike, then offered to drive me home.). OK, on to the black. I did the helmet, gloves, shorts, and skates in black. I also used black for the colored part of the eye — I didn't think baby blues would work too well for a rough and tumble hockey player !

Here is a closer view of the "cut" on the hockey player's face.

After the black dries, paint the white side stripe on the shorts. The helmet looked a little boring, so I took some white paint, making sure the brush was rather dry, and applied some various shapes to the helmet (an ear pad and an upper and lower separation). This should be very subtle, almost like a shadow.

A hockey puck makes a perfect stand for our hockey player! This is a great project for the hockey player in your life—paint the jersey to match their team colors and add their name to the back to really make it personal! Makes a great gift and can be adapted for other sports as well.

Gallery

Santa

The Man ("Dad")

The Butterfly Lady

The Ice Hockey Player

Grandma and her knitting basket.

Laura the Nurse and Larry the Chemist

Uncle Tony and the "Is it really morning" Lady.

Happy
the
Clown.

Buz the
Croquet
Player

Thomas the
Pasta Chef
with his
assistant
Rosetta.

The Gang: Patch, Chester, and Mortie.

A. Charles (Chuck) Artinian.

The "real" Chuck Artinian, model for the carving shown at the left.